NO BISCUITS IN HEAVEN

A modern day church mystery play for radio

Ruth Finnegan

NO BISCUITS IN HEAVEN

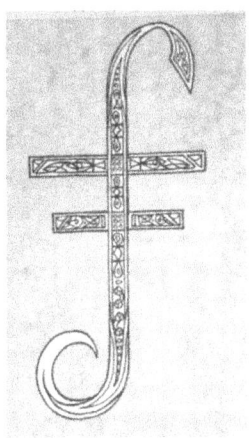

2020

ISBN 978-1-71666-451-9

Callender Press

Old Bletchley

www.callenderpress.co.uk

CAST

Narrator
God
Little angel
Mary ("Mirri")
Old gentleman
Old woman
Cross mother
Whining boy
Street sleeper
His dog
Helpful woman
Tantrumming little girl
Harassed mother
Kind woman
Woman getting out of bus
Second helpful woman
Gruff bus driver
Rule-keeping bus driver
Bullying young man
Kindly bus driver

Lady car driver
Minister

Sundry voices
  Passers by
  Supermarket people
  Bus passengers
  Church attenders

NO BISCUITS IN HEAVEN

A MODERN-DAY MYSTERY PLAY

FADE-IN MUSIC (ORGAN)

NARRATOR And God called the naughty little angel to him, and spoke thus.

GOD (sadly) You know don't you ... what you have done

LITTLE ANGEL (even more sadly) Yes (pause) I know I have to leave heaven.

GOD You do.

LITTLE ANGEL Forever?

GOD We-ell ....

 LITTLE ANGEL. Is there no way back?

GOD Mmmm. If you perform 70 times 7 tasks (firmly, hearing the gasp of dismay) Yes.

LITTLE ANGEL Not 70 times 7!! 7 would be quite bad enough. *SEVEN.*

 GOD (laughing) bargaining you rascal ? Well, maybe. In one day.

LITTLE ANGEL   Three days, you could never do it in one.

GOD We-ell.

PAUSE

LITTLE ANGEL   (shyly) What are the tasks?

GOD To observe and count sevent- er, seven acts of real goodness.

LITTLE ANGEL *Real* goodness? On *earth*??! (silence) How will I know?

GOD You will know.

LITTLE ANGEL Well, um ... oh but clothes. Earth. Wings no good.

GOD When you are there, you will have the right clothes.

LITTLE ANGEL Oh.

GOD Just leave your halo here.

LITTLE ANGEL My *halo!* no *NO*, not parting with that, most precious possession. *Never.*

 GOD Oh well (affectionately, to himself) Little rascal. (to the little angel) Off you go brat .

 (to Mary) can't help being fond of the rascal y'-know. 'll be back d'you think Mary?

MARY (Irish accent) Better be an' all, just see to it, you. Keeps us lively up here, the wee mischief. Like our silly goats, *so* much more fun than the goody goody sheep.

GOD (reproachfully, trying not to laugh)) Oh Mirri! (pause) er, um, know what you mean. Not so bad y'self.

MARY (affectionately, sound of kiss) Mmm.

   SOUNDS OF SLITHERING, FLAPPING
   WINGS, WIND, FRIGHTENED SQUEAKS,

WHEEEEEEE

THUD. BUMP-BUMP. SUBDUED SCREECH

LITTLE ANGEL *Ohhh*! *Bang*! Oh look at me!
jeans with tears in, tee shirt,. Cool. Er, no jacket,
COLD. *Brrrrr.* (pause) wonder when lunch ...
(pause) um, how 'bout food? Hm, what 'm I sup-
posed to do now? *Brrrrr*

SOUNDS OF ANGEL'S TIMID HESITATING
STEPS ON PAVEMENT, AND CHATTERING
BRISK-STEPPING PASSERS-BY

SOUND OF OLD WOMAN'S FOOTSTEPS,
SLOW ...

LITTLE ANGEL Oh, what a heavy basket that
old woman's carrying (pause). Look at her, an'
why's no one helping?

SOUND OF SHUFFLING FOOTSTEPS, STICK,

That old gentleman's much too old to help her.
wish *I* - but she'd just think I was going to mug
her. Oh dear, maybe I *should* try.

OLD GENTLEMAN That looks heavy, let me help you my dear, I'll carry it, it's too much for you.

OLD WOMAN But your walking stick ...

OLD GENTLEMAN I'll manage. Please allow me, it will be an honour.

SOUND OF SLOW DOUBLE STEPS GOING OFF

LITTLE ANGEL (ecstatically) Done it done it, *ONE*!

SOUND OF LIGHT DANCING FOOTSTEPS

LITTLE ANGEL Now what. Walk on. Very very observant.

SOUND OF TWO LOTS OF DRAGGING STEPS ON PAVEMENT (ADULT WITH YOUNG CHILD)

CROSS WOMAN Come *along* sonny we're late.

BOY (whining) I'm hunnnngry...,

CROSS WOMAN You can jus' wait till your'n home.

BOY (whine whine)

CROSS WOMAN (extra crossly) Here then, biscuit, last one, was keeping for myself, all ri' , just
go slow wi' it now.

BOY Mmmm, choc bikky.

SOUND OF CRUNCHING, ONE BITE

BOY Look, what's that man doing sitting with a
dog an' a cap in front' of him? Hullo nice doggie,
lovely lovely aren't you soft and beautiful

SOUND OF LOW SNARL

STREET SLEEPER 'is name's Billy.

CROSS WOMAN (shortly, to boy) it's a dirty
street sleeper, keep away. Two meters, Germs.
Oh oh, take care son, nasty dog. (pause)I Hm,
we'd better give 'I'm wee bitty money 'case he
curses us, (sound of her searching jungly coins
in purse) hm just have our bus fare. Mm. Okay
we'll walk home,

SOUND OF COINS DROPPING INTO CAP

A' course he'll spend it all on - well never you mind. What those people really need is food not cash you know, allus hungry they say.

STREET SLEEPER (African accent) Yes ma'am, always hungry. Starving. Now (engagingly) if that young man there were to give me a bite 'o ' is biscuit ...

BOY.Ohhh,(pause) ohh - oh all right here y'ar, it's real nice. Have it. I'll just lick chocky bits off my finger (sound of sucking), oh yes, look other hand too (more sucky sounds)

STREET SLEEPER You're an angel y'are. Yum. I'll have one bite, an then - 'ere Billy me boy, this is for you.

LITTLE ANGEL Nice doggie, you liked that didn't you?

SOUND OF HESITANT FOOTSTEPS

LITTLE ANGEL Oh dear, no more people with loads. *Where* can I find 'good deeds'? oh this is *so* hard. Only ONE kind deed so far, oh dear

CROSS WOMAN He's much too good good to that dog-cur of his if you ask me. Fancy passing on your bikky to *it. What a* waste!

CLOCK STRIKES TWO

GOD's VOICE (very quiet, almost from within the little angel, his inner insight) Didn't you see any-thing just now?

LITTLE ANGEL What *here*? On the *street*? (pause) Oh oh. *Yes, I see.* She did well 'spite of all her crossness. Giving the biscuit (*I* would have liked it, chokky one). Oh and the dog . And the cross woman walking home, not bus fare. *Wow. Yes.* Can't really believe it - *here*, on *earth*! but yes hurray*, TWO.*

SOUND OF SKIPPING FOOTSTEPS... SLOW-ING DOWN. STOPPING

SUDDEN HOOTS, TYRE SQUEALS, BRAKES,
SKIDDING , SHOUTS

VARIOUS OVERLAPPING VOICES *Look out!*
Ohh! Oh *no*. Thrown himself in front of the bus.
Pushed his friend out of the way. Saved him.
Dead? Sure to be.

LITTLE ANGEL Well I don't know what *you* think
almighty God-up-there, but *I'd* say that was an
act of real real goodness (pause) Didn't you
see? An' you said once 'what greater good can
any man do than to lay down his life for his
friend?'. Well he *did*. I'm counting it whatever
you say. (defiantly) *THREE*. So there! (to self) oh
dear, have I got that right, er, three, halfway,
well, well nearly, maybe I'll be back in heaven in
time for lunch after all. Ohh, what's - ?

SOUND OF AMBULANCE SIREN, RACING
ENGINE, VEHICLE STOPPING WITH JERK,
STEPS RUNNING OUT

VARIOUS OVERLAPPNG VOICES

Ambulance.

They'll take care of things.

He's dead.

Yes, but his friend who saved him .. ah getting him onto a stretcher.

Great paramedic, looks so young. Yeah just a girl ...

LITTLE ANGEL Oh God look at her face, she's so so tired, on duty since dawn do you think?
(pause) But that's her *job* innit, so not a 'good deed', doesn't count. Shame.

PAUSE

GOD Do you not think dear child to count a *life* of service ? .

LITTLE ANGEL *Saving* a li... ? Oh, *her* life? Would that count? A *life* of goodness?

GOD Why not?

LITTLE ANGEL Aaah! Well that's, mm, lost count, doesn't matter. If only I wasn't so cold and hungry.

SOUND OF DRAGGING FOOTSTEPS, FIERCE COLD BLASTS OF WIND , SUDDEN STOP

LITTLE ANGEL Ohh! What's this? on pavement. Ha, sixpence! SIXPENCE!

SOUND OF SCRAPING COIN OFF PAVE-MENT

LITTLE ANGEL Now for a - for a wherever you buy a biscuit, ooh I'm so so hungry? Excuse me madam where can I get a biscuit?

SOUND OF FRIENDLY LAUGHTER

HELPFUL WOMAN Supermarket, round the corner silly kid, 50 yards..

LITTLE ANGEL '*Super*'-market. Too good for me then now I'm down here below. But - oh, I *need* a bikky. (pause) I'm a very tired little angel. And (repressed sob) my feet are so sore, *horrible* earth shoes.

SOUND OF TIRED BUT DETERMINED FOOTSTEPS. ... SLOWING,

CLOCK STRIKES THREE

LITTLE ANGEL *Now* I can get something to eat.but - is sixpence right entrance fee? Will they ... um, I'll sneak in.

SOUND OF ENTERING SUPERMARKET

GENERAL SUPERMARKET SOUNDS

LITTLE ANGEL Oh dear, all those people push- ing around not keeping their distance? and I bet they've, oh, *viruses*. Oh sorry sir, er I'm just look- ing just ah looking. Biscuits y'know, bikkies.

MORE SUPERMARKET SOUNDS, FOOT- STEPS

Ah, here. (sound of paper scrunching). Can't get the manna - or I think they call it packet here not proper language - to open up so how do I get just one? Need longer nails (whispering) like Sata- has, ooh ooh hope nobody's listening? Maybe someone can help - oh goodness!

TANTRUM YELLS, SOUND OF TODDLER THROWING HERSELF ON FLOOR, SCREAMS

Oh look at that ! Yah yah noises,   little girl in - I think they call it 'tantrum' here -   all over the floor, oh dear mother wits end, embarrassed embarrassed embarrassed... What on earth will happen now}?

KIND WOMAN (to the mother) Don't worry. We've all been there! Know what it's like. Just a stage, don't worry (laughing) terrible twos. Thing is to distract her. (suddenly! to the child) Ohh ohh look, *what's that*?

SLIGHT PAUSE IN TANTRUM YELLS, THEN RESUME

MOTHER (gloomily) *Knew* it wouldn't work..

LITTLE ANGEL Wonder if - , what can I, if I , my, oh, my halo . Look here little girl, here here here, yo yo yo yo yo, look spinning, hoop, rainbow colours, look, yo yo yo .

CLINK CLINK CLINK Of HOOP (HALO) SPIN-NING ALONG FLOOR

SOUND OF LITTLE FEET RUNNING AFTER HOOP, LIFTING IT UP, LAUGHING IN TRIUMPH

LITTLE GIRL Got it!

LITTLE ANGEL (to self) Good thing was in my pocket, my halo, my preciousest... . But, well - no good here, not like oh (stifled sob) in heaven.with G-God. (to the little girl), do you like it then?

LITTLE GIRL Me like. (firmly) Me have.

LITTKE ANGEL (gulp) Look, all right you have it. (pause) Just take it quick.

MOTHER Say thank you nicely Katey.

LITTLE GIRL (little voice) Sank you.

LITTLE ANGEL (encouragingly)   Come on then Katey girl, look, you carry the biscuits for me, come on then. Oh we-e-ell done!. Good girl!.

SOUNDS OF CHECKOUT AND LEAVING THE STORE

OVERLAPPING VOICES 'Bye. Thanks. Got yr bikkies okay? See you.

LITTLE ANGEL That kind kind woman. No fun having a tamtam toddler. Embarrassing. Ha, FOUR. Or er, is it five? I'm so tired, don't even know *where* I am by now.

SOUND OF SLOW TIRED FOOTSTEPS ON HARD PAVEMENT, AFTER A WHILE WITH SLIGHT LIMP

LITTLE ANGEL And it's so cold, thought it'd be hot here. Like hell. *Brrrrrrrr* .

SOUND OF SHIVERING, SHAKING, CHATTER-ING TEETH

SOUND OF BUS DRAWING UP AND STOP-
PING

WOMAN GETTING OUT OF BUS Thanks dri-
ver, good. You keep yr bus nice an' warm I'll say
that f'you , bye now, thanks.

LITTLE ANGEL Oh, warm! (timidly) Is it *really*
warm in there lady?

WOMAN 'course. Wot on earth you doing' this
freezing weather in just a tee shirt? Left yr jacket
at 'ome?

LITTLE ANGEL 'ome, er, home,oh oh I'm so
homesick.

WOMAN How ' bout a bus to get you then
(pause).stuck for the fare, oh well (JINGLE OF
COINS) look here's a shillin' , all coppers but
they'll be okay. 'Nuff to take you 'ome.

LITTLE ANGEL Oh oh *thank you.*

WOMAN (calling) Bye now, safe 'ome.

LITTLE ANGEL Oh, *home*!

SOB. SOUND OF RAIN

LITTLE ANGEL. She's right. I don't want to go anywhere "cept home. Heaven. It's so cold and wet here - an' *shoes* are *awful*. It's not fair. Is bus *really* warm? stand by bus stop, that's right isn't it.

SOUND OF BUS ARRIVING, DOOR OPENING

GRUFF BUS DRIVER (singsong, with satisfaction) Full up full up no room full up full up.

SOUND OF DOOR CLOSING, BUS LEAVING

LITTLE ANGEL Ohh (sob, shiver)

CLOCK STRIKES FOUR

SOUND OF ROUGH HEAVY FOOTSTEPS

BULLYING YOUNG MAN Out uv me way you.

SOUND OF LITTLE ANGEL BEING SHOVED
VIOLENTLY AGAINST THE BUS STOP

LITTLE ANGEL Ohh! Yes of course sir, sorry sir, I was only waiting -

BULLYING YOUNG MAN (violently) Waiting you say, *waiting.* An' jus' look at you, rags, Ha, another immigrant, bogus asylum seeker the lot o' them (hiccup) yeah bogus, cluttering the streets.. Littering. *Outa my way*, are you deaf?

LITTKE ANGEL Sorry sir (ppause, then very timidly) Are you ... ?

BULLYING YOUNG MAN Don't bug me you, just outta me way, din' y' hear me?

SOUND OF ANOTHER PUSH

BULLYING YOUNG MAN Last bus today this is! Need ta get ova t' me girlfren' to - ha (aggressively) none o' your business.

LITTLE ANGEL (aghast) Last today? Will, will there be room? Sorry sir.

BULLYING YOUNG MAN (hiccup) There'd betta be,

SOUND OF BUS DRAWING UP, DOOR OPENING

DRIVER Just one, first in queue, that's you young un, hop in.

LITTLE ANGEL Th-thank you, thank goodness. I - here's (proudly) my fare. Here?

SOUND OF COINS DROPPING INTO MACHINE

DRIVER Take your ticket (to bullying man) sorry sir, no more allowed.

BULLYING YOUNG MAN Bloody hell I'm coming.

SOUND OF VIOLENT PUSH

DRIVER No you don't. Ouch.

SOUNDS OF PROTESTS AND FRIGHTENED SQUEAKS FROM PASSENGERS

LITTLE ANGEL Look look I don't need ... I, I mean his need is greater.

SOUND OF ANGEL GETTING OUT HASTILY

FALLING THE LAST FEW FEET

BULLYING YOUNG MAN *Now* you're talking young un.

DRIVER But ...

BULLYING YOUNG MAN Shut yr mouth black-man .

LITTLE ANGEL Funny thing to say, wha does he ... ? Nice really I'm sure when you know him properly. Whatta lot to learn down here.

BULLYING YOUNG MAN (calling out) Y'are no s'bad then kid, bit uv an angel really, ta then ...

SOUND OF DOOR SHUTTING   (CUTS OFF END OF HIS WORDS), THEN OF BUS START-ING AND DRIVING AWAY, FADING INTO DIS-TANCE

LITTLE ANGEL No more buses he said.
(pause) Mm, if I just walk and walk, and walk and walk, and ... then maybe it'll get back to heaven. Home. Long way. (pause). It *must* be seven good deeds by now. That nice man just

now, looked rough outside but good deed really,
talked to me normal just as if I was a real person.
Off I go ...

SOUND OF DRAGGING FOOTSTEPS,
MARKED LIMP, OCCASIONAL GASPS AND
STIFLED MOANS OF PAIN

SOUND OF FOOTSTEPS STOPPING

LITTLE ANGEL (sleepily) I, I can't ... My feet are
so sore.

SOUND OF HOOT, BUS PASSING

LITTLE ANGEL Oh, *not* last after all, run run
run ... Run ...

SOUND OF DESPERATELY RUNNING FOOT-
STEPS, PANTING, STOPPING

,SOUND OF DOOR OPENING, CLOSING, BUS
LEAVING WITH A CHEEKY HOOT

LITTLE ANGEL Oh, missed it, didn't run fast
enough, I'm useless. And I'm *freezing.*(pause)
Come on Angel, WALK!

SOUND OF STUMBLING FOOTSTEPS

CLOCK STRIKES FIVE

LITTLE ANGEL (trying not to cry) Tramp, tramp tramp, such a long day . Oh, ohh! And I said three, *one* day awful enough tramp, tramp.

MUSIC TO SHOW TIME PASSING, AGAINST SOUND OF FOOTSTEPS, SLOW, LIMP ...

UNEXPECTED STUMBLE OFF KERB

LITTLE ANGEL Ohh! Oh dear ..

DRAGGING FOOTSTEPS ALONG ROADWAY, DECIDED LIMP, HARDLY MOVING NOW

LONG SOUND OF HORN, SOUND OF CAR DRAWING UP, BRAKES, STOPPING

LADY DRIVER You're in the road, *do* look out. Hm, you look in a bad way (pause, no answer). Can I give you a lift? You look very tired and cold.

LITTLE ANGEL Oh oh lady, I'd *love* a lift.

LADY DRIVER Where are you making for?.

LITTLE ANGEL I, I want to get to heaven, but (sob) I've lost the way, I don't know where I am, I don't know ... and ...

LADY DRIVER Well jump in and we'll see.

SOUND OF CAR DOOR OPENING, LITTLE ANGEL SINKING INTO SEAT SIGH OF RELIEF, DOOR SHUTTING , CAR SETTING OFF

LADY DRIVER What's your name then?

LITTLE ANGEL. Christy miss, er ma'am.

LADY DRIVER Christy - ah?

LITTLE ANGEL Just Christy.

LADY DRIVER So where do you live Christy?

LITTLE ANGEL. (firmly) At home (confused, after a pause), well usually. Just now I ... .

LADY DRVER(laughing, not taking it seriously) Wanting to get back to heaven (sigh) Don't we all.

LITTLE ANGEL (very seriously) *Yes.*

They drive on for a time in companionable silence.

LADY DRIVER I'm for the City Centre Church,
the one they call the Church of Christ the Cornerstone, the one, you know, with a dome and a
cross you can always see on top. Evening service.

LITTLE ANGEL I, I, I'm not really a church person but ..., If that's where you're going.

LADY DRIVER (laughing) Well if you looking for
heaven the shopping centre's just opposite. I'll
just pop round the back of the church, free park-
ing on Sundays and evenings.

LITTLE ANGEL (in a little voice) Yes, no.

SOUND OF CAR STOPPING

LADY DRIVER Here we are then, hop out and we'll go round to the front opposite the shopping.

APPROPRIATE SOUNDS

LITTLE ANGEL Could I just sit inside the door miss out of the wind? My feet are too sore to reach the shops, and I don't really ...

LADY DRIVER C'mon then.

SOUND OF CHURCH DOORS OPENING AND THEM GOING IN,

LADY DRIVER (to reception people) This is Christy. Visitor.

OLD GENTLEMAN (at reception - from the first good deed) You're very welcome Christy.

Here's today's Order of Service and a hymn book for you.

LITTLE ANGEL I don't really ...Oh, it's you. (shyly) I , I saw you helping that old lady,

OLD GENTLEMAN Mm, oh that? Oh nothing. Reminded me of my wife that's all.

LITTLE ANGEL Is she here sir?

OLD GENTLEMAN (pause) Waiting for me in heaven. (to incomers, variously) Good morning Robert, how's Susan by now? Hullo my dear are you here for the children's playgroup, that's great then, Teresa here will lead you out with the candle when - Oh Agnes, how lovely are you all right now? It's a blessing to see you back. (to Little Angel) We're very pleased to welcome you here Christy, first time? Make yourself at home, one way to heaven this is.

LITTLE ANGEL Ohh!

SOUND OF PEOPLE GOING IN

OLD GENTLEMAN Just go on in to the worship area, yes straight through the doors there. (Interrupting himself repeatedly to greet and be greeted by more incomers) How was the Cruise Peter? There'll be some fun hymns today, young Christy, jazzy ones most to your liking, I guess, classical music too if you like that. (interrupting again) Good morning Ron, ah yes big print hymnbook for you, just a minute, here you are ....
(SLOW FOOTSTEPS AS HE GOES IN) (to Little Angel) always a special blessing to have him with us (Pause) Yes. Bach, piano, organ. (interrupting)l Hi Ladipo, don't forget your hymnbook sir, no you're in plenty of time (SOUND OF HURRYING FOOTSTEPS GOING IN) (to Little Angel) Always thinks he's late that one bless him. Superb organist we have, choir too today, you'll see,,

LITTLE ANGEL I, I don't know. I'm not the sort of - ..

LADY DRIVER Oh come on. Look, we'll go in together.

LITTLE ANGEL But but my clothes ...

LADY DRIVER (laughing) Ho ho, just wait till you see some of the others, you're fine compared to them. Well (laugh) some of us like to dress up a bit, good excuse, fun, but - oh come on, who cares what we're wearing. Mind you the Ghanaian robes are real something, just you wait.

LITTLE ANGEL Ghanaian?

OLD GENTLEMAN 's great to have all sorts coming - doctors, teachers, paramedics -

LITTLE ANGEL Ohh! Maybe her?

OLD GENTLEMAN Yes ambulance people when they're free (work so hard), nurses too (the same) and midwives, IT nerds shop workers, young uns like you w' their own groups, old uns like me, an' oh, *anyone.* Oh yes, and little kids as well, special things for them.

LADY DRIVER (sotto voce, a bit cynically but with a smile underneath) Just as well too!

MUTED SOUNDS OF PIANO STARTING UP INSIDE

LADY DRIVER. Hi, young un, look at that raga-muffin family jus' coming in, great attenders they are. Feel better?

LITTLE ANGEL (reluctant laugh) See what you mean, oh all right, just for a minute. Will (nervous) will the leaflet tell me what's happening, what I should be doing?

 LADY DRIVER 'course. Not that any one minds.

SIUND OF FOOTSTEPS OF TWO PEOPLE GOING IN. SUDDEN SLITHER TO A STOP, TURNING BACK, RUNNING, SOUND OF SUDDEN HALT.

OLD GENTLEMAN Got you. (very kindly). What's the matter, why are you running away?

LITTLE ANGEL (panicking) OH oh. it says here (RUSTLE FROM LEAFLET) - and I haven't got any.

OLD GENTLEMAN Where? (MORE RUSTLES) Oh when people give gifts? (very seriously). Listen dear friend from heaven (SOB from little angel), as we all are, your *presence* here is your gift, what more could anyone ask. (another SOB). Go in to this new beautiful world, let your heart be high .

LADY DRIVER (from inside) Come on in my dear, I'm just here.. We can sit at the back just in front of the toddlers with their toys.

SOUND OF HESITANT FOOTSTEPS,

CLOCK STRIKES SIX

FOOTSTEPS OF MINISTERS AND ASSIS-
TANTS GOING PAST DOWN THE AISLE,
SWISH OF LONG ROBE

LADY DRIVER (whispering) Excuse me, oh it's
you Mabel are you all right? could me and my
friend just squeeze past. Thanks so much. Bless-
ings.

SOUNDS OF SQUEEZING PAST, THEN TWO
PEOPLE SITTING DOWN

CHOIR STARTS

Rutter, "The lord bless you and keep you"

LITTLE ANGEL (trying not to sob) I, I think it's me
they're blessing.(shakily) As good as heaven.

FADE OUT

TIME PASSING MUTED SOUNDS (PIANO,
ORGAN, SINGING, WORDS)

FADE IN

MINISTER ... always. Go in peace to love and serve the lord.

CONGREGATION (raggedly) In the name of Christ amen.

SOUNDS OF PEOPLE COMING OUT INTO THE VESTIBULE, GREETING EACH OTHER, ORGAN IN DISTANCE

VARIOUS VOICES Good service.

Yes nice story and the reading, quite funny about the pharisees and ...

Sermon rather moving, so personal and simple and full of thought.

Mm, didn't agree with everything he said , but who does? Made me think. Um, maybe I *did* nod off a wee bitty at one point, but well who cares, heard the start ...

LADY DRIVER (to Little Angel) Staying for coffee? Do!

LITTLE ANGEL I don't drink coffee. Will there be - ?

LADY DRIVER Tea? Yes a' course, and maybe a biscuit (laugh) if you're good.

LITTLE ANGEL (very seriously, shamefaced) I'm *not* good, that's why ...

LADY DRVER Oh nonsense, none of us are and (chuckle) I can tell you we all enjoy the biscuits! (seriously) Churches are for *imperfect* people like us y'know. We *try* to be better of course. But who's *really* good in this here life of ours? You don't have to be good to come to church, it's for people like us, oh come on. Everyone's quite friendly.

SOUNDS OF CLINKING CUPS, CHATTER ETC.

LITTLE ANGEL. Not perfect, no but - all those *good* people I met.

OLD GENTLEMAN Looking very cheerful all of a sudden, y'are, (grinning) quite angelic-like. Well, *be* an angel then and give me an arm to the coffee, by my age the legs get tired standing around.

SOUND OF CAREFUL, FOOTSTEPS (QUIET ON WOODEN FLOOR), CHATTER AND CLINK OF CUPS GETTING CLOSER

FADE OUT / FADE IN

GOD (whispering) Well?

LITTLE ANGEL Yes, *lots* good deeds, not just seven, see? 70 times 7, more. Maybe you won't believe it but yes, truly... (pause, then rushing on, bravely) God, would you mind very very much if I stayed here? I like it here because they're imperfect just like me (pause, then timidly) I lost my halo Lord, an' it got dented from falling on the floor and ...

GOD (laughing) Mine too, it's all spikey and thorny by now (smiling), old and comfortable. (pause) You *gave* it away didn't you.

LITTLE ANGEL (very guiltily) Yes Lord, I did. This, this little girl wanted .... and I - Sorry.

GOD So, you see, there *are* good deeds on earth.

LITTLE ANGEL Yes, her mum ...

GOD (carefully) Yes indeed my dear beloved little angel.

 LITTLE ANGEL (shy but persevering, determined to get through it) I like it here. I like this Church of Christ the Cornerstone (bet you don' know what that means Lord, *I* do!); and they put up with me even though I AM just a little fallen angel, and, and, would you believe, they *let me help pour out the tea*, an' an' *didn't mind when I spilled it.*

SOUND OF SLOSH FOLLOWED BY GENTLE LAUGHTER FROM SEVERAL PEOPLE

They just laughed and wiped it up. Please let me stay, please. I would like to dwell among them. And er ...

SOUND OF CRUNCHING BISCUIT.

GOD (laughing) No biscuits in heaven you mean rascal?

SOUND OF GOD AND MARY CHUCKLING

LITTLE ANGEL We-ell, I'm not perfect am I. Just *trying* ....

FADE OUT TO GENTLE CHATTER AS CLOCK STRIKES SEVEN

NARRATOR And God smiled and was content. He looked and he saw that the world he'd created was very good.

MUSIC (BACH PIANO, PROLONGED)

SLOW FADE OUT

THE END

www.ingramcontent.com/pod-product-compliance
Lightning Source LLC
Chambersburg PA
CBHW071119220526
45467CB00004B/1956